STARTERS
LONG AGO
BOOKS

Cooks and Kitchens

Macdonald Educational

hare

peacock

Long ago the Romans had feasts.
Romans lay on couches around the table to eat.
2

flamingo

swan

The Romans ate many kinds of meat.
We do not eat many of these things today.

hot stone

water

clay oven

The first men did not know how to cook.
They ate raw food.
Then they discovered how to make fire.
They could boil or bake food.
Hot stones were used to boil the water.

4

mixing dough

loaf

flour

Everybody made their own bread.
There were many different kinds.
Many people ate dark brown bread.
White bread was made for rich people.

People picked fruit in summer.
They made it into preserves.
Jam is a kind of preserve.
This was one way of storing fruit.

10

meat

salt

barrel

These people are salting meat.
They put the meat in barrels with salt.
Salt meat keeps for months.
People stored meat this way in winter.

In winter people sometimes made
an ice pit under the ground.
They put ice and snow into a hole.
They hung the meat above the ice.
The cold kept the meat fresh.

12

fennel   chickweed   rosemary sage marjoram

parsley

This woman is picking some herbs.
Sometimes meat was not fresh.
People used herbs and spices
when they cooked it.
The herbs and spices hid the bad taste.

13

1. skimming the cream

2. churning

3. patting

This is how butter was made.
Many houses had a dairy.
Dairymaids made the butter from cream.
They made it in a churn.

14

Most water was too dirty to drink.
So people made other drinks.
In many countries people made wine.
They made the wine from grapes.

dog

mechanical spit

Meat was roasted on spits over a fire.
At first, boys turned the spits.
Then people made machines to turn them.
One machine was worked by **a dog**.
16

electric oven

electric ring

Here is one of the first electric cookers.
It was used about a hundred years ago.
People were scared of it at first.

pulley
rope

dining room

lift
shaft

kitchen

This kitchen is in the basement.
The dining room is upstairs.
So the cook put the food in a lift.
Then she pulled a rope and the food
went up in the lift.
22

Most people went to church on Sundays.
They took their food to the baker
on the way to church.
He cooked it for them in his big oven.

23

Everybody used to eat at home.
Then a cook in France had a new idea.
He opened a restaurant.

People came to eat at his restaurant.
They paid him for their meal.
Soon there were many restaurants.
The chef did the cooking.
The waiters served the food.

white paper

sticky tape

You can make a chef's hat out of paper.
Cut out the shapes in the picture.
Fasten them together with sticky tape.

lid

paper

cream

See if you can make butter out of cream.
Shake the cream in a jar like this.
It will take a long time,
so ask your friends to help you.

27

Index